|| ||| || ||||| ||| |||| || |||
D1095730

DEC 0 8

MX Bikes

Evolution from primitive street machines to state of the art off-road machines

John Perritano

x1000r/min

CRABTREE PUBLISHING COMPANY
www.crabtreebooks.com

Crabtree Publishing Company

www.crabtreebooks.com

Coordinating editor: Chester Fisher
Series and project editor: Shoreline Publishing Group LLC
Author: John Perritano
Series Consultant: Bryan stealey
Project Manager: Kavita Lad
Art direction: Rahul Dhiman
Design: Ranjan Singh
Cover Design: Ranjan Singh
Photo research: Akansha Srivastava
Editors: Adrianna Morganelli, Mike Hodge

Acknowledgments

The publishers would like to thanks the following for permission to reproduce photographs:

p4: Joachim kohlen Duetsches Zueirad/ NSU Museum; p5: Mary Evans Picture library/Photo library; p6-7: Simon Cudby; p8: Racer X Archive; p9: Racer X Archives; p10: Ake Jonsson/Terry Good Collections; p11: Ake Jonsson/Terry Good Collections (all); p12-13: Motorcycle Museum Hall of Fame; p14: Joël Robert Archive/Terry Good Collections (all); p15: Joël Robert Archive/Terry Good Collectons; p16: Terry Good Collections; p17: Racer X Archive; p18: Terry Good Collections (all); p19: Terry Good Collections (all); p20: Terry Good Collections; p21: Terry Good Collections (all); p22: Francis Kuhn; p23: Francis Kuhn (top); p23: Racer X Archives (bottom); p24: Francis Kuhn (all); p25: Francis Kuhn (all); p26: Gary Newkirk/Getty images (top); p26: Paul Buckley (bottom); p27: Paul Buckley; p28: Racer X Archive; p29: Racer X Archive (all); p30: VINCENT VAN DOORNICK/AFP/ Getty images; p31: Paul Buckley (top right); p31: Jeff Gross/ Getty images (bottom)

Cover and title page image provided by Paul Buckley

Library and Archives Canada Cataloguing in Publication

Perritano, John
    MX bikes / John Perritano.

(MXplosion!)
Includes index.
ISBN 978-0-7787-3988-3 (bound).--ISBN 978-0-7787-4001-8 (pbk.)

    1. Trail bikes--History--Juvenile literature. 2. Motorcycles, Racing--Juvenile literature. 3. Motocross--Juvenile literature. I. Title. II. Series.

TL441.P47 2008   j629.227'5   C2008-901518-5

Library of Congress Cataloging-in-Publication Data

Perritano, John.
    MX bikes / John Perritano.
      p. cm. -- (MXplosion!)
    Includes index.
    ISBN-13: 978-0-7787-4001-8 (pbk. : alk. paper)
    ISBN-10: 0-7787-4001-3 (pbk. : alk. paper)
    ISBN-13: 978-0-7787-3988-3 (reinforced library binding : alk. paper)
    ISBN-10: 0-7787-3988-0 (reinforced library binding : alk. paper)
    1. Motocross--History--Juvenile literature. 2. Trail bikes--History--Juvenile literature. 3. Motorcycles, Racing--Juvenile literature. I. Title.
    GV1060.12.P474 2008
    796.7'56--dc22

          2008008945

Crabtree Publishing Company

Published in Canada
Crabtree Publishing
616 Welland Ave.
St. Catharines, ON
L2M 5V6

Published in the United States
Crabtree Publishing
PMB16A
350 Fifth Ave., Suite 3308
New York, NY 10118

Published in the United Kingdom
Crabtree Publishing
White Cross Mills
High Town, Lancaster
LA1 4XS

Published in Australia
Crabtree Publishing
386 Mt. Alexander Rd.
Ascot Vale (Melbourne)
VIC 3032

Contents

Gottlieb Daimler's "Bone Crusher"

Motocross racers use skill and daring to race over dirt tracks or take to the air to perform freestyle tricks high above the cheering crowd. But they wouldn't be able to ride anywhere without specialized motorcycles. And they can, thanks in part to a German engineer!

Gottleib's Got It!

Gottlieb Daimler never saw motocross superstar Ricky Carmichael rocket down the sandy ruts of Southwick in Massachusetts. Nor did he ever see James "Bubba" Stewart master the Unadilla track in New York. Still, Daimler would be pleased if he attended a motocross (or MX) race today. If it weren't for this snappy-dressing German engineer with the balding head and white beard, motocross might not exist. Daimler didn't invent the sport, yet many credit him with inventing the first motorcycle in 1885.

From Bike to Motorbike

Born in 1839 near Stuttgart, Germany, Daimler would later become one of the top automobile makers in the world. In the late 1800s, the only engines available were powered by steam. Daimler and others wanted to come up with a more powerful engine powered by gasoline. They tried lots of different models, and finally locked in on the use of pistons. These moved up and down in the engine to turn a shaft, which would turn wheels. These engines were the first to be small enough to put inside something to make it go.

Where are the tires? This early motorized bicycle got its nickname, the "bonecrusher," for the less-than-soft ride that it gave its users.

Daimler's group went on to put the engine into carriages, which turned, over time, into today's automobiles. Before he became famous for making cars, however, Daimler motorized a bicycle. Other engineers had previously toyed with fitting steam engines to bicycles. Daimler went one step further. He took the gasoline-powered engine that was developed by Nikolaus August Otto and put it on a wooden-framed bicycle known as the "bone crusher." The bone crusher had iron wheels in front and back. As the rider moved the bike, the wheels rattled the rider. Daimler's motorbike included two small wheels on the outside of the bike. The motorcycle was born.

Two Wheels

While Daimler's "bone crusher" had four wheels, other engineers had tried to design a two-wheel model that worked. The bikes, however, always tipped over. In 1892, the Millet became the first two-wheeled motorbike. The bike had an engine in the hub of its rear wheel. Once people began riding motorcycles, it didn't take long for racing to begin. Eventually, these two-wheeled carriages would thrill millions of motocross fans. The sport of motocross itself **evolved** out of races in England in the 1920s.

Daimler worked with other inventors to put the world on wheels. He later founded a car company with Otto Benz— a company that eventually became the world famous Mercedes Benz.

Moto Fact

The first engineers to develop the first practical two-wheeled **production** motorbike were the Hildebrand brothers of Munich, Germany. The Hildebrand brothers built the Motorad, which had a top speed of 25 miles per hour (40km/h).

MX Bike Parts

In motocross, riders seldom go for blazing speed alone in choosing a bike. Mostly, they want to make sure that the machine's engine can pull the rider and the bike over hills and through mud.

From the Ground Up

The tires on a motocross bike look nothing like the tires on a street motorcycle do. The treads are rough and chunky for better traction on dirt surfaces. The braking system on a motocross bike has to be dependable and **durable** because racers continually apply their brakes going into turns. Shock absorbers on the back and front tires cushion the ride. They let the **frame** of the motorcycle move up and down over bumps, instead of landing with a thud like on the old-time "bone crusher."

MX Bikes

Although motocross bikes look and perform differently, their basic anatomy is the same.

Exhaust Pipes:

Once the fuel burns, the exhaust pipes release waste gases into the atmosphere.

Drive Chain:

The drive chain transfers power from the engine and gearbox to the rear wheel.

Foot Peg:

Foot pegs are located on both sides of the bike.

Seat:

Although riders seldom sit when racing on bumpy and hilly courses, the seat is fashioned from padded foam.

Throttle:

Racers use the throttle to control the power of the engine.

Fuel Tank:

Fuels tanks are designed not to rupture during a crash.

Rear Shock Absorbers:

Shock absorbers soften the bounce and thud that riders feel.

Front Shock Absorbers:

The front shock absorbers are located in each of the front **forks** of the bike. The forks attach the bike frame to the front wheel.

Engine:

The engine is the powerhouse of the bike. It is mounted high above the ground for good clearance.

The Engine

It doesn't matter whether you're Jeremy McGrath, Travis Pastrana, or Chad Reed. If your bike doesn't have a good engine, you're not going to win a race. The engine is the motorcycle's power plant.

From Gas to Go!

Here is how a typical motorcycle engine works: fuel is mixed with air. That mixture is pulled into the bike's motor. The fuel is sprayed into the top of the **cylinder**. A **spark plug** fires and ignites the fuel. *Kabooom!* An explosion occurs. The force of that explosion causes the engine's pistons to move up and down. As that happens, the pistons turn a crankshaft. The crankshaft converts the up-and-down motion of the piston to a circular movement. That circular motion, along with a gearbox and chain, moves the rear wheel. The rider, using the throttle, controls the flow of fuel and, thus, the speed of the bike.

Two-stroke engines are light yet powerful, making them perfect for dirt bikes.

Engine at Work

Zooooom! The motorcycle is off and running. Motorcycle engines come in two designs—two-stroke engines and four-stroke engines. Originally, most motocross bikes were four-stroke engines. A two-stroke engine, however, produced more power than a four-stroke engine of the same capacity. The engine capacity is measured in **cubic centimeters**, also known by the initials "cc." Cubic centimeters measure how large the cylinders in the engine are.

How a Two-Stroke Engine Works

Fuel and air is sucked into the motor as the piston moves up the cylinder. A spark plug ignites the fuel. The resulting explosion moves the piston down the cylinder. As burned gases pass through the bike's exhaust system, more fuel flows above the piston. As the new fuel flows above the piston, the piston moves up again.

Steve Lamson's Honda CR 125 is powered by a two-stroke engine.

Early MX Machines

With the birth of motocross in England, riders needed a new type of motorcycle to handle the challenges of MX. Smart designers came to the rescue.

British Scramblers

While all motocross bikes are built in generally the same way, not all bikes are created equal. The evolution of motocross bikes mimics the evolution of the sport itself. Bikers began racing on dirt tracks in the 1920s, when the British **scramble** was born. The early bikes looked nothing like the high-tech, sleek machines of today. The bikes weighed as much as 400 pounds (181.44 kg) and had virtually no shock absorbers to smooth out the bumps, dips, ruts, and holes of the early racecourses. The bikes were four-stroke beasts—heavy and difficult to handle. Often, racers would get off of their bikes in the middle of the race to push their machines through a mud hole. No one had yet designed a motorbike for such tough riding.

The British made the first motorcycles that were used in the off-road races that became today's motocross. Here's a rider moving smoothly over a dirt road riding an early British model.

The First Scramblers

The first bike that was produced just for scrambles came off of the **assembly line** in 1930. Built by the Husqvarna Company of Sweden, the Specialracer Motocykel was popular with racers and engineers. Other European companies soon began developing scramble bikes of their own. These new racing bikes were stronger and could better deal with dirt, rocks, and bumps. The seats were wider and more comfortable. Riders used their feet to shift gears instead of taking one hand off of the handlebars. By the mid-1940s, engineers began designing faster motocross motorcycles. The two-stroke engine changed the face of the sport. Previously, four-stroke engines powered all motocross bikes. The two-stroke engines made the bikes easier to handle and much faster.

Early off-road motorcycles were made for riding on dirt, but owners had to spend hours keeping them clean to run well.

Moto Fact
Four-stroke engines do not pollute the air as much as two-stroke engines do.

Known as the "Husky," the Swedish-made Husqvarna bikes challenged British power. They were designed to ride over rough roads.

The Rickman Metisse

As motocross grew in popularity, certain bikes began to define the times in which they were raced. Many of those bikes pushed the boundaries of technology and style. In the 1950s and 1960s, Europe was still the hub of motocross racing. The British, in particular, ruled the sport. The British manufacturers, such as Triumph and BSA, were proud of their bikes. But these bikes were heavy. A Triumph 500 Trophy, for example, weighed around 300 pounds (136.08 kg). Other bikes tipped the scales at 340 pounds (154.22 kg). Figuring that heavier bikes weren't always the best performers, Don and Derek Rickman began to rethink what a motocross bike should be.

The brothers experimented with **hybrids**. They took the best that each manufacturer had to offer and combined it to build their own creation. As the 1950s ended, the Rickmans had designed a new bike that would set the standard for motocross machines. The brothers called their creation the Metisse Mk 1. The brothers built several variations of the Metisse over the years.

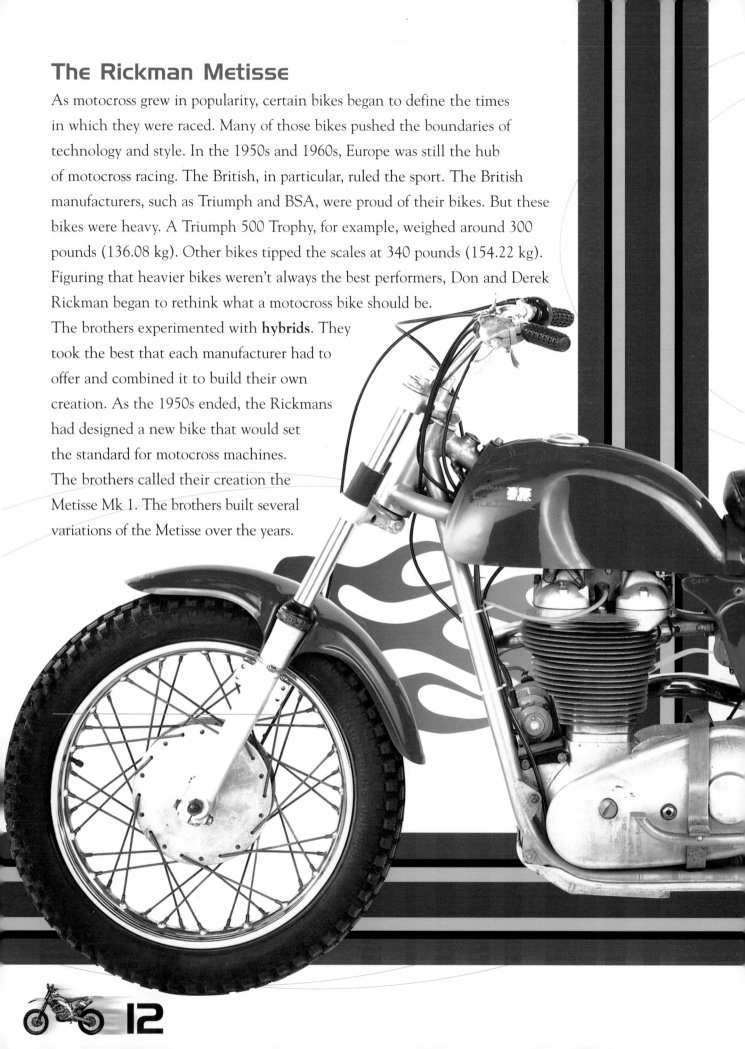

The Metisse is a Winner

The Mk 3 Metisse was the bike that put the Rickmans on the motocross map. Historians describe the bike as revolutionary in both design and style. The Rickmans crafted the bike from materials that were lighter and stronger than anything previously available. The nickel-plated frame weighed only 24 pounds (10.89 kg). The Metisse's lightweight fuel tank, two-piece seat, and rear mudguard flowed seamlessly together, creating an **aerodynamic** fit that cut down on wind resistance. With the Metisse, the Rickmans rewrote the book on motocross motorcycle design.

The Rickmans Ride Again

At the 1960 MX des Nations in France, the British team of Don Rickman, Jeff Smith, and Dave Curtis took home the top honors. Rickman, of course, rode his Metisse **mongrel**. Two years later, the British team that included the Rickman brothers took second place. The top gun of the race? The Metisse. The Metisse would be part of winning teams in 1963, 1964, and 1965. The Metisse became popular with other riders, including the Belgian and Swiss teams.

Moto Fact

Metisse is the French word for mongrel. A mongrel is a dog that has many breeds among its ancestors.

Apart from the Metisse, the Rickmans also made frame and body kits for competition off-road bikes like Montesa and Zundapp, and sports bikes such as the Rickman Hondas. They also made Matchless roadracers and the Triumph Metisse which was used mainly for desert racing in the U.S.A.

Hail the Two-strokes

By the mid-1960s, heavy British four-stroke engines, like the ones in the Metisse, were slowly losing their appeal. It was time to change to lighter and faster two-stroke engines.

Two from the East

In the early 1960s, the Czechoslovakian CZ factory began producing several two-stroke models that eventually helped kill the four-strokes. By 1962, CZ had produced two-stroke 250cc bikes with twin exhaust pipes that did well in competition. A year later, Vlastimil Valek won the opening moto of the Czech 500 Grand Prix riding a 263cc bike. It was the first time that a two-stroke had won in the 500cc class. Although the bellowing four-stroke engines would still be around for a while, Valek's win turned the motocross world on its ear.

At the annual World Championships, Belgium's ace, Joël Robert, was a regular on the winners' stand. His all-around skills let him win titles in several classes of motorcycle racing.

Joël Robert won races all over Europe throughout his career. Here, he's shown flying over a course in Switzerland.

Joël Robert Rocks!

In 1964, one of the world's most gifted riders showed again how much better the CZ two-strokes were. Belgium-born Joël Robert rode a CZ and became the youngest-ever 250cc champion. The 20-year-old eventually won six 250cc World Motocross Championships, his last coming in 1972. While several riders would come close to equaling Robert's record—Roger DeCoster won five championships—Robert was far and above one of the best riders of his day.

Born to Race

When Joël Robert's father saw his new son in 1943, he declared, "We will make a rider out of him!" By the age of two, Joël could take apart sections of a motorcycle and reassemble them. He won his first race at the age of 17—not by finishing first, but by finishing . . . only! The race, on a boggy, hilly track, was stopped after three laps when Joël was the only rider to make it up the largest hill. Though he won his first world title in 1964 on a CZ, he switched to a Japanese-made Suzuki in 1970. He won another world title, the first by a rider using a Japanese bike. After retiring from racing holding numerous world records, Robert became a manager for the Belgian national MX team. He's also, naturally, in the Motorcycle Hall of Fame.

Moto Fact

East Germany's Paul Friedrich tallied the first of his three consecutive 500cc titles aboard CZ two-strokes.

Already a legend in his home country, Joël Robert added to his amazing list of career accomplishments when he came to America. Here, he rests between races at Saddleback in 1975.

Moto Fact

Joël Robert's record stood for 31 years until Stefan Everts scored his seventh world championship in 2003.

Husqvarna Comes to America

Although the CZ was popular in the United States, it couldn't match the eye-popping excitement of the Swedish-built Husqvarna. The Husqvarna, or "Husky," will be forever linked with the arrival of big-time motocross in the United States.

Here Comes the Swedes!

Americans have engineer Edison Dye and rider Torsten Hallman to thank for bringing the Husky and competitive motocross to the States. Dye believed that he could create a demand for the Husky by showing Americans what motocross looked like in Europe. Dye also wanted to demonstrate how well the Husky performed against the machines raced by American riders. He hired Swedish riding superstar Torsten Hallman, who had just won his third 250cc World Motocross Championship, to hold exhibitions on the West Coast.

Huskymania

In 1966, Hallman's appearance really jump-started America's love of motocross. American fans and riders marveled at Hallman's riding abilities. The press wrote glowing articles about Hallman and his Husky. Thousands flocked to see the Swede ride. A year later, Dye brought more European riders to the United States, including Joël Robert and Roger DeCoster. Dye paid the Europeans to ride in his Inter Am Series. The 1967 Husky that Hallman rode as he **barnstormed** with his European friends was sleek, strong, and durable.

Swedish star Torsten Hallman roars right into your lap in this action photo taken during his awesome MX career.

The Husky's Brief New Life

The Husky's only national title in the 1970s came in 1976 by rider Kent Howerton. His mechanic, Eric Crippa, had modified the bike with several custom parts. Those changes made Howerton a champion. As luck would have it, the "Rhinestone Cowboy," as Howerton was nicknamed, couldn't defend his title the following year. His Husky often had mechanical problems. In fact, Howerton didn't score a single win in 1977. Suzuki signed Howerton the next year. He would go on to win 32 major AMA events over his career and is still ranked as one of the top-10 motocross riders of all time.

Moto Fact

By the end of the 1960s, Husqvarna had increased its production from 300 bikes per year in the mid-1960s to 3,000 bikes by the end of the decade.

American star rider Kent Howerton was one of several U.S. riders who rode Huskys. Here, he's at a Saddleback Park Trans-AMA from 1975.

Made in Japan

By the early 1970s, motocross was becoming a popular motor sport in the United States. But European bikes were too expensive, clunky, and unreliable for American riders. A new player in the game emerged when Japanese-built motorcycles came to town.

Better . . . and Cheaper!

Led by Suzuki, Yamaha, Honda, and Kawasaki, the Japanese began vying for their place on the racetrack. The Japanese built better bikes that were more reliable, cheaper, and easier to ride than the European and American models were. Not only was the styling and performance of the bikes better, but the Japanese also produced more bikes than anyone else. If you were an American and wanted an off-road machine, there was no shortage of inexpensive and competitive bikes made in Japan.

The Elsinore CR250M

One of the first Japanese machines to thrill Americans was Honda's Elsinore CR250M. With its sleek aluminum fuel tank, gray sidecovers, and compact foot pegs, the CR was a rider-friendly machine. The Japanese named the bike after a small town in California that had hosted an annual off-road Grand Prix. To help sell the CR, Honda landed U.S. national 250-class winner Gary Jones as the team's top rider. Jones switched from riding Yamahas. It didn't take long for the 1973 edition of the CR250M to catch on.

(below) The Honda Elsinore CR250M was the class of the field among early Japanese MX bikes. Many top riders hopped onboard once it debuted.

(above) One of the first Japanese companies to make MX bikes was Suzuki, but they quickly found themselves eating dirt behind the faster, better Hondas.

Amateur riders quickly became serious motocross racers. The Elsinore had its problems, though. Its gearbox caused problems. And because of its 57-inch (144.78-cm) length, the CR turned slowly. Still, the CR did well at high speeds and outperformed any MX Yamaha or Suzuki of the time. Yamaha, however, was not content with letting Honda lead the way in performance and styling. Yamaha eventually built its YZ model, which outperformed the Elsinore. Within a year of its release, the CR250M had become a "second-string" racer.

Gary Jones was the Yamaha team's top rider, helping the company and its bikes attract new groups of American fans and riders.

The Monoshock, modeled here by Swedish rider Hakan Andersson, was made by Yamaha to join the revolution in new bikes in the 1960s.

Here Comes Yamaha

The jet engine revolutionized air travel. The telephone revolutionized the way that people communicated over vast distances. In 1974, Yamaha revolutionized motocross with new and better motorcycles and engines.

YZ? Why Not?

In 1974, Yamaha launched two production bikes, the YZ250B and the YZ360B. Yamaha outfitted each with its monoshock, or "monocross" suspension system. A **suspension system** is important to how a vehicle brakes and handles. What made this system different than that of other bikes? The monocross gave the YZ more **horsepower**, better braking, and a better system to handle the bumps of the road. Riders—at least those who could afford the expensive bike— flocked to the YZ. Yamaha officials knew, however, that while the YZ outperformed other bikes, the company couldn't make any money by producing only a few of the bikes. By 1975, the YZ began to fade, and Yamaha's other monoshocks, the MXBs, began to emerge as the machine of choice. Most of today's bikes use the monoshock system that was pioneered by the YZs.

20

What is a Suspension System?

Cars, trucks, and motorcycles all have suspension systems. Using springs that are attached to each wheel, this system helps the vehicle ride smoothly over rough surfaces. Compared to a car or a truck, a motorcycle's suspension system is relatively simple. The front suspension system consists of a pair of tubes on the fork, or the part that holds each side of the wheel. In the back, a single **swingarm** has one or two shock absorbers. The swingarm pivots in an up and down motion. That allows the suspension to absorb the bumps in the road. In Yamaha's monoshock system, only one shock absorber connects the rear swingarm to the motorcycle's frame.

Swedish star Torston Hallman rode this Yamaha prototype motorcycle at this World Championship race in the early 1970s. Hallman was a leader in bike development.

Torton Hallman made his first mark riding a Husqvarna, helping it become a big part of the sport. But he moved on to Yamaha and helped them create this prototype.

The Golden Age Begins

Thanks to even hotter and faster Japanese bikes and awesome American riders, the 1980s saw motocross, especially among American riders and fans, rise to new heights of popularity.

Changing Times

By the time that 1980 rolled around, motocross had changed dramatically. The Europeans and their giant bikes were out, and the American riders and the more competitive Japanese bikes were in. In 1980, Suzuki began the year with Howerton and Mark Barnett winning championships in the 250cc class and 125cc class, respectively. For its part, Honda and Chuck Sun captured the AMA's 500cc title in 1980. But bigger things were on the horizon. At this time the pack was filled with future Hall of Fame riders. Many experts consider this period of time to be the glory years of American motocross. On any given day, you'd be able to watch riders such as David Bailey, Mark Barnett, Broc Glover, Jeff Ward, Rick Johnson, and Johnny O'Mara—all legends of the sport. At the same time, the decade signaled the end of Bob Hannah's reign over American racing. It was time for new faces to take the lead.

Mark Barnett rode Hondas to several championships, including titles won on both small and large motorcycles.

David Bailey and the Honda RC500

David Bailey had pretty big shoes to fill when he began his motocross career. After all, his stepfather was Hall of Famer Gary Bailey. In 1982, legendary racer Roger DeCoster hired the younger Bailey to race for Team Honda. In 1984, Honda designed the RC500 so that Bailey could race the bike in the AMA's 1984 500cc Motocross Championship. The bike's **chassis** was handmade. Designers had also placed the fuel tank lower on the frame to give the rider better balance. Bailey faced Yamaha's defending champion Broc Glover that year. Glover didn't stand a chance. Bailey and the RC500 won the first eight of 10 races. Glover wouldn't go down without a fight, winning the last two races. It was too little too late. Bailey and the RC500 had won the title.

(above) Chuck Sun won the "big" 500cc class in 1980 riding a Honda.

(below) Honda racer David Bailey accepts yet another trophy for a big win.

Jeff Ward's KX250

In 1985, Jeff Ward was one of the hottest racers around, beating some of the best motocross racers of the time on the sleek-looking KX250. This exotic factory special had a handmade frame and swingarm, and a lightweight aluminum gas tank. Ward's success that year began in the final round of the AMA Supercross Championship. Riding the Kawasaki green machine, Ward bested five-time motocross champ Broc Glover. Later on, Ward took second place during the AMA 250 Motocross Championship, beating Johnny O'Mara by two points.

David Bailey was one of the top riders of the 1980s. Here he is in action in 1983 at the Washington D.C. Supercross, one of many events that he won in those years.

Clear the way! During a mud-spattering ride at the Lake Sugartree track in Virginia, here are riders Jeff Hicks (21), David Bailey (6), Ricky Johnson (5), and Ron Lechien (2).

International Success

A few weeks later, Ward rode a 250 during the Motocross des Nations. He dominated the 250 class to help the Americans win. While 1985 was the first year that Ward raced the 250, it would also be the last year for this special factory-made bike. Ward's 1985 Kawasaki was the last of the great "works" bikes. Production machines were now becoming more common on the motocross circuit. In 1986, new rules restricted changes to the MX motorcycles, ending an era where "works" bikes, or handmade bikes specially built for MX racing, dominated the sport.

Other Gear Gets Safer

While the motorcycles got better, so did the gear that riders wore. They always used helmets, but new materials like fiberglass, Kevlar, and carbon made the helmets both lighter and safer. Chest protectors, shin guards, and face shields made of heavy-duty plastic also added safety.

Moto Fact

Ward's 250 title was the first AMA 250 National Motocross Championship for Kawasaki.

David Bailey felt right at home as he churned through the dirt on a Bultaco bike at his home track at Lake Sugar Tree in Virginia.

A young David Bailey gets ready for another motocross race.

Modern Bikes

As the 1990s dawned, motocross solidified itself as one of the most popular motor sports in the world, and particularly in the United States.

McGrath's Honda

Mention supercross, and one racer that comes quickly to mind is Jeremy McGrath. Now, mention a legendary bike, and McGrath's Honda CR250 might be the first machine that pops into your head. Although most race fans are familiar with McGrath winning races on a Yamaha, the Honda CR250 helped turn McGrath into a legend of the sport. In 1993, McGrath exploded onto the MX scene, winning 10 races aboard a two-stroke, steel-framed Honda CR250. McGrath's 1995 CR250 was one of the last steel-framed 250s that was manufactured by the company. Honda, along with the other Japanese manufacturers, would eventually move to aluminum chassis on their motocross models.

Jeremy McGrath reached great heights— really!—riding a Honda CR250.

Four Times a Champ

Many racers, including McGrath, didn't like the transition from steel to aluminum. McGrath was hesitant to mess with a winner. He eventually won four supercross championships for Honda, as well as the 1995 AMA Motocross Championship. He switched to Suzuki in 1997, losing that year to Kawasaki's Jeff Emig. But McGrath continued to be a big part of the motocross scene. In the 1990s, the birth of the X Games gave him new ways to show off his skills. McGrath and other riders took part in the different events at the action-sports-packed X Games. These included freestyle and Supermoto and Step-up. In that last event, riders zoomed up a ramp one at a time and competed to see who could reach the greatest heights. The bikes had to change to succeed in these new events.

Here's McGrath on his Honda taking part in the X Games' Supermoto event in 2007.

The Four-strokes Come Back

The more things change, the more they stay the same. Even as two-stroke engines dominated, new rules and laws sent engine makers back to the drawing board.

Four-strokes Get a Break

While the 1970s and 1980s showed the dominance of the Japanese two-strokes, the 1990s marked the return of the four-stroke engine. The return of the four-strokes began when several state governments, including California, began passing laws that were aimed at protecting the **environment**. Those rules basically banned two-stroke engines from road and open-course competitions, such as desert races. The two-strokes burn fuel poorly, putting out too many fumes, and harming the environment. Although motocross was spared from these regulations, bike makers began to focus on a new generation of cleaner-burning, four-stroke machines.

Doug Henry's Revolution

The real return of the four-stroke engines came with Doug Henry's historic win aboard a Yamaha YZ400F prototype at the 1997 season-ending Supercross in Las Vegas. That win was the first time that a four-stroke had ever won an AMA Supercross race. Many racing historians consider his win to be the beginning of the current four-stroke revolution. A year later, Yamaha wanted Henry to ride its YZ400F all the time. It was a difficult decision for Henry to make. He had been in several crashes and been injured, and it took a while for him to prove himself once again on the motocross circuit.

Doug Henry rode this Yamaha YZ400F prototype to a major victory in 1997.

Henry's High Point

Racing an unproven motorcycle didn't fit into Henry's professional racing plans. In 1998, Henry became the first rider to win an AMA 250 Motocross Championship on a four-stroke. His win proved that the newly engineered four-strokes were successful racers. The revolution had begun. The four-strokes would dominate the sport within a few years.

Tough Ending

After his triumphs in the late 1990s, Henry switched to riding more often in Supermoto. He had a lot of success there as well, earning new fans and friends. Unfortunately, he was badly injured in a crash during a practice run in 2007 and had to retire from racing. The popular and much-loved Doug Henry was elected to the Motorcycle Hall of Fame in 2005.

The success of Doug Henry on four-strokes like this model helped spark their return.

A great personality and winning skills helped make Henry one of the top racers of recent years.

High Tech from Austria

Japanese motorcycles had been all the rage for years, but in the 1990s, a new source of great bikes emerged. Though it's not known as a motocross hotbed, Austria became the home of the world's hottest bikes.

KTM Arrives

In 1934, a small automotive repair shop in Austria began making motorcycles at a rate of three a day. Today, that motorcycle manufacturer is often on the cutting edge of motorcycle technology, dominating several classes of MX racing. KTM—short for the company's name in German, Kraftfahrzeuge Trunkenpolz Mattighofen—got into MX in a big way beginning in the early 1980s, when Austria's Heinz Kinigadner took the 250cc World title in 1984. By the 1990s, the company had unveiled its new-generation four strokes. In 1999, Kelly Smith almost took a KTM to victory at the St. Louis Supercross. KTM finally won its first AMA-sanctioned race in 2000, when Smith won aboard the Austrian brand at High Point Raceway in Mt. Morris, Pennsylvania.

A Legend Returns

KTM hired Stefan Everts in 2006 to become the company's motocross race director. It was a major hire for KTM. Everts, a Belgian, had 10 world championships and 101 Grand Prix victories in his 18-year career. Known for his smooth style and effortless riding, Everts had a choice to join the Yamaha team or KTM. In accepting the KTM job, Everts said he was looking forward to helping KTM's young riders get to the next level both physically and technically.

Stefan Everts finished his career on Yamahas, but he was quickly scooped up as an adviser by KTM.

What's next?

As motocross continues to grow in popularity, MX bikes will continue to evolve and improve. Engineers will constantly tinker with bike designs and engines to find that perfect combination of power, speed, and handling. These bikes will be faster, sleeker, and more fun to watch. And who knows? You might be a winner riding one.

Ready to race: no matter what bike riders use, they're ready to speed to the front of the pack!

Supermoto Action!

Supermoto is a cross between motocross and road racing. Supermoto bikes are generally single-cylinder, four-strokes with wheels that top out at 17 inches (43.18 cm). The rear tires are often hand grooved to allow for better acceleration on the dirt portions of the supermoto courses. Supermoto bikes can handle a crash well. Riders are often able to re-enter the race after taking a spill. That's what happened to Jeremy McGrath during the 2005 X Games. At the time, Chad Reed grabbed the holeshot and led for the first two laps with Doug Henry not far behind. As Henry looked for a way around Reed, Jeremy McGrath motored through the field. He found himself on the floor on the second lap, however. The King would not be denied. He spent the next 32 laps chasing Henry and Reed. McGrath and his Honda came in second. Had he had a few more laps to go, The King might have won first place.

Glossary

aerodynamic How air flows over a surface. Engineers design aerodynamic bikes to reduce wind drag in order to increase fuel efficiency and speed

assembly line A line of production in which a number of assembly operations are performed in a set sequence

barnstorm To travel and perform stunt shows

chassis The metal skeleton of a motorcycle or car

cylinders The tube-shaped sleeves that house the pistons in an engine and where the fuel/air mixture is drawn in to be burned

durable Able to last

environment One's surroundings

evolved Changed over time

frame The skeleton-like structure of a motorcycle on which the various components that make up the bike are mounted

horsepower A measurement of an engine's power

hybrid A mixture of different elements

production Manufacturing of a product

prototype An experimental or new version of something

scramble Early motocross event in Great Britain

spark plug A device that ignites the fuel/air mixture that is sprayed into the cylinder

Index

32

Printed in the U.S.A.